D0517907

sweet dreams, Moon Baby

A Quilt to Make, a Story to Read

Elly Sienkiewicz

C&T PUBLISHING

©2003 Eleanor Patton Hamilton Sienkiewicz
Editorial Team: Darra Williamson, Kerry I. Smith,
Gailen Runge, and Diane Kennedy-Jackson
Proofreader: Eva Simoni Erb
Cover Designer: Kristy A. Konitzer
Design Director/Book Designer: Kristy A. Konitzer
Illustrator: Mary Ann Tenorio
Production Assistant: Jeffery Carrillo
Photography: Photos on pages 4 and 18 by Katja Sienkiewicz
Photos on pages 5 and 19 by Sharon Risedorph
Other photos by Diane Pedersen unless otherwise noted

Published by C&T Publishing, Inc., P.O. Box 1456, Lafayette, California, 94549

Front cover: *The Moon Baby Quilt*, detail

All rights reserved. No part of this work covered by the copyright hereon may be reproduced or used in any form or by any means—graphic, electronic, or mechanical, including photocopying, recording, taping, or information storage and retrieval systems—without written permission of the publisher. The copyrights on individual artworks are retained by the artists as noted in *Sweet Dreams, Moon Baby*.

Attention Copy Shops: Please note the following exception—Publisher and author give permission to photocopy pages 33–36, and 44 for personal use only.

Attention Teachers: C&T Publishing, Inc. encourages you to use this book as a text for teaching. Contact us at 800-284-1114 or www.ctpub.com for more information about the C&T Teachers Program.

We take great care to ensure that the information included in this book is accurate and presented in good faith, but no warranty is provided nor results guaranteed. Having no control over the choices of materials or procedures used, neither the author nor C&T Publishing, Inc. shall have any liability to any person or entity with respect to any loss or damage caused directly or indirectly by the information contained in this book. For your convenience, we post an up-to-date listing of corrections on our web page (www.ctpub.com). If a correction is not already noted, please contact our customer service department at ctinfo@ctpub.com or at P.O. Box 1456, Lafayette, California, 94549.

Trademarked (™) and Registered Trademark (®) names are used throughout this book. Rather than use the symbols with every occurrence of a trademark and registered trademark name, we are using the names only in the editorial fashion and to the benefit of the owner, with no intention of infringement.

Library of Congress Cataloging-in-Publication Data

Sienkiewicz, Elly.
  Sweet dreams, moon baby: a quilt to make, a story to read / Elly
Sienkiewicz.
    p. cm.
  ISBN 1-57120-209-9 (paper trade)
  1. Appliqué--Patterns. 2. Quilting--Patterns. I. Title.
  TT779.S548 2003
  746.46'041--dc21
                          2003010175

Printed in China
10 9 8 7 6 5 4 3 2 1

Cray-pas Specialist®, Pigma Micron®, and Gelly Roll® are registered trademarks of Sakura of America.
Ultrasuede® is a registered trademark of Toray Ultrasuede (America), Inc.
Magic Sizing® is a registered trademark of Faultless Starch/Bon Ami Company.
Colorfast Printer Fabric™ Sheets is a trademark of June Tailor, Inc.
Clover® White Marking Pen is a registered trademark of Clover Mfg. Co., Ltd.
Baltimore Beauties® is a registered trademark of Eleanor P. H. Sienkiewicz.

Contents

The moon like a flower
In heaven's high bower,
With silent delight
Sits and smiles on the night.

William Blake, *Songs of Innocence*, 1789

Dedication

This book is dedicated to Elias Emerson Sienkiewicz, my moon baby become grandchild. He was born March 12, 2001 in Concord, Massachusetts, to my son Donald and his beloved wife Katja. Elias's sister, Little Ellie, not yet two years old, awaited his birth with great expectations.

To Wee Elias,

Sweet magical child, you sang to me before you were born. I felt your presence, a welcome beneficence. Your spirit's closeness surprised me, infused me with joy. Because I worked on this quilt, perhaps, I came to think of you as the baby in the moon. I would look for you of a night, see a cherubic lunar face, and smile.

You were newborn a week, when I first held you. To me your features were exquisite, and your visage a bit ancient and wise. You touched my soul, left me in awe. A modern grandmother, my home is far from yours. Yet when I stitch on this quilt, I am closer to you. Soon I will finish, and the quilt will become yours. Like the quilt's layers, our spirits, too, are stitched together, leaving no distance between us. Know that in my heart I will always be grateful that moonbeams brought your magic to live among us. Sweet joy befall thee!

Wee Elias with his sister, Little Ellie.

Acknowledgments

Thank you to my dear friend Mary Sue Hannan (Sue), who provided a 1930s newspaper illustration, the inspiration for my design for the baby-asleep-in-the-moon center medallion. Sue designed a complete quilt around the babe by bordering the medallion with pieced stars. She encouraged me to appliqué designs in the centers of the stars, which prompted me to write *The Moon Baby Story*.

Thank you to Jean Wells, whose piecing method for *The Sawtooth Star Quilt* is so clever that Sue wanted to sew stars.

Thank you to Holly Sweet, whose technical care and authorship underlies this book's piecing instruction.

Thank you to Mona Cumberledge, whose hand quilting brought *The Moon Baby Quilt* to life.

Thank you to Kay Thompson Summit and Lynda Carswell, who made original quilts using the Moon Baby patterns. Thank you also to Charlene Dakin, who made the darling nursery accessories.

Thank you to my dear daughter-in-law Katja Sienkiewicz, for her photographs of Ellie and Elias, Davina Teresa, and me.

Thank you to Irwin Bear of P&B Textiles for producing my Baltimore Beauties designer fabrics, from which I designed *The Moon Baby Quilt*, and for generously providing the fabrics for both *The Moon Baby Quilt* and to incorporate into other projects in this book.

And finally, thank you to Darra Williamson, Gailen Runge, and all the fine folks at C&T Publishing who worked skillfully to make this book itself a work of art.

Before
I was born,
I sailed
the dark sky,
Asleep in a crescent moon.

Love was the ocean
            that rocked me,
Stars were my
guardians and guides.

The sun
touched my face
each morning,
I smiled in its warmth at noon.

Evening's cool breath
rustled my hair,

8

Night's dark
brought my spirit to
bloom.

The sun rose
in the morning,
The moon rose at night.

There was **dawn**
on my left; then
dusk on my right.

The sun, the moon,
and the stars were my friends,
Constellations the stories I knew.
Yet I longed for a life
on the earth...

For a **father** to hold me,

A **mother** to care,
A **sister** to laugh with and **love**.

When dawn
became dusk
And dusk became dawn,

My dream at last came true.

I was **born** to this
life dear **family**,

Loving and
loved by you.

The Moon Baby Quilt:
★ An Invitation to Take a Journey ★

Take a wonderful journey as you make *The Moon Baby Quilt*. This charming heirloom combines hand appliqué, whimsical embellishments—including embroidery, oil pastel stencil shading, and inking—and machine piecing.

You can use needleturn appliqué techniques (pages 25–28) and several fancywork embellishments (pages 30–32). However, for quick and easy results, consider edge-fused appliqué (pages 28–29) or freezer paper-inside appliqué (page 28), combined with your own embellishments. To add a special touch, try the Ultrasuede technique (page 29).

The easiest patterns are presented first. Therefore, when you appliqué the patterns in the order in which they appear on pages 33–36, beginning with The Shooting Star and ending with The Moon Baby and Sprinkled Stars, you'll get a fine review of the delights of appliqué, beginning with plain and ascending to fancy. As you stitch, think of your own special child, and the stitches—as though by magic—will join your souls. I suspect that by the time you've appliquéd the star centers and the center medallion, you will quite magically have memorized the story as well. Soon after, you'll be holding your sweet baby wrapped in the quilt, telling the story as little fingers touch your stitches in wonder.

Instructions for making *The Moon Baby Quilt* begin on page 37. On page 40 you'll find

The Moon Baby Quilt, 50" x 50". Made by Elly Sienkiewicz and Mary Sue Hannan. Quilted by Mona Cumberledge.

inspiration for making the quilt in an alternative color scheme. Use any combination of the Moon Baby appliqué patterns to incorporate into a quilt with a different set, such as Lynda Carswell's *Golden Slumbers* on page 42. You can even use your favorite Moon Baby appliqués to personalize and embellish accessories for the nursery. See pages 43–47 for inspiration and directions.

For general quiltmaking instructions, refer to a comprehensive basic quiltmaking book such as *The Art of Classic Quiltmaking* by Harriet Hargrave and Sharyn Craig (see Sources on page 47). Best wishes for a happy journey!

Getting Started

Tools and Notions

My father-in-law was a Russian immigrant and a carpenter. Though his English was poor, his wisdom—"With right tools, you can do anything"—was clear, and applies to appliqué, too. The right scissors, needles, thread, and marking pens make appliqué easy.

Thread & Embroidery Floss

50 to 60 weight 100% cotton or cotton-covered polyester thread, color-matched, for appliqué and piecing

Six-strand cotton embroidery floss for most embroidery

Pearl cotton #5 for The Moon Baby's hair

Needles and Pins

Milliner's #10 needles for appliqué

Embroidery/crewel needles (mixed-size package) for embroidery

Ball-headed straight pins—short for appliqué, long for piecing

Marking Pens & Pencils

Sakura Pigma Micron .01 permanent acid-free pen, in black, to inscribe or mark on light to medium fabrics

Sakura Gelly Roll Metallic Silver or Metallic Gold or Clover White Marking Pen to mark on dark fabric

Fine-lead mechanical pencil to mark on light fabric

Oil Pastels

Artist-grade oil pastels such as Sakura Craypas Specialist for stencil shading appliqué edges. The pigment is in the oil; thus, top-quality oil pastels cost more.

Template Materials

$8\frac{1}{2}$" x 11" sheets of uncut, self-stick labels, available at an office or copy store, for photo-copying patterns. Alternatively, trace patterns onto freezer paper.

Scissors

Good 5" scissors for appliqué

Good 5" scissors for cutting paper templates

Fine embroidery scissors for turning points

Rotary Cutting Tools

Rotary cutter

18"-long ruler (including $\frac{1}{8}$" increments marked in both directions, and angle markings)

Cutting mat

Sewing Machine

To machine piece, you need a machine with a reliable straight stitch. To machine appliqué (page 28), you need a zigzag feature. To make a pillow (page 45), you also need a zipper foot.

Iron

A hot iron (cotton setting) for the freezer paper-inside appliqué method

Fusible Web

Lightweight fusible web for edge-fused, hand or machine appliqué. **Note:** Do not use self-stick web for hand appliqué.

Miscellaneous

Round toothpick to turn under edges for needleturn appliqué

3" embroidery hoop

Glue stick for Ultrasuede appliqué

Clear tape to repair cut made in window template

5" x 5" muslin scrap and paper tissue pressing cloth (for stencil shading)

Masking tape (3/4"-wide) to use as a guide for inscribing words onto fabric by hand

Optional

June Tailor Colorfast Printer Fabric Sheets for photo transferring words and images

Lightbox to transfer patterns onto paper and fabric

Dressmaker's tracing paper to transfer embroidery lines onto fabric

Selecting Fabrics

Determine your color scheme and select prewashed, 100% cotton fabric for your quilt. Choose a dominant color for the background and star centers, a secondary color for the star points and inner border, and scraps of various colors for the appliqués.

As an option, you can use Ultrasuede for some of the appliqués. Ultrasuede is machine washable and can be pressed with a steam iron on the low (synthetics) setting. Test the Ultrasuede for colorfastness. See page 29 for additional guidance in working with this product. If your local quilt or fabric shop does not carry Ultrasuede, refer to Sources on page 47.

Yardage Requirements

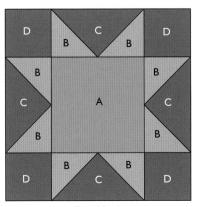

Star block

All yardages are based on 42"-wide fabric. You may wish to add a little extra to allow for shrinkage.

Dark-blue print: $2\frac{1}{8}$ yards for the setting triangles (G, H, and I), and background for the stars (C and D) and center medallion (E)

Assorted blue prints: scraps (at least 7" x 7") to total $\frac{2}{3}$ yard for 11 star centers (A)

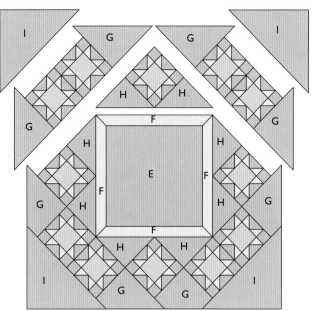

The Moon Baby Quilt layout

Pink print: 7" x 7" scrap for 1 star center (A)

Assorted gold and yellow prints: $\frac{1}{3}$ yard for the medallion frame (F), $\frac{2}{3}$ yard for the binding, and scraps to total $\frac{1}{2}$ yard for the star points (B)

Assorted blue, pink, yellow, gold, orange, red, green, and flesh-toned prints and solids: 6" x 6" scraps for the appliqués

Pale blue print: 2 yards for the backing

Thin, polyester batting: 54" x 54"

Optional:
Ultrasuede: 3" x 3" scraps in browns, reds, greens, yellows, golds, and flesh-tones for the appliqués

Fusible web: $\frac{1}{4}$ yard lightweight for machine appliqué

Cutting

From the dark-blue print, cut
48 rectangles, $2\frac{1}{2}$" x $4\frac{1}{2}$", for the star backgrounds (C).

48 squares, $2\frac{1}{2}$" x $2\frac{1}{2}$", for the star backgrounds (D).

1 square, 21" x 21", for the center medallion background (E).*

2 squares, $16\frac{5}{8}$" x $16\frac{5}{8}$". Cut each square in half diagonally in both directions to make a total of 8 outside setting triangles (G).

2 squares, $12\frac{5}{8}$" x $12\frac{5}{8}$". Cut each square in half diagonally in both directions to make a total of 8 inside setting triangles (H).

2 squares, $16\frac{3}{8}$" x $16\frac{3}{8}$". Cut each square in half diagonally in one direction to make a total of 4 corner triangles (I).

From the assorted blue prints, cut
11 squares, 7" x 7", for the star centers (A).*

From the pink print cut
1 square, 7" x 7", for 1 star center (A).*

From the assorted gold and yellow prints, cut
96 squares, $2\frac{1}{2}$" x $2\frac{1}{2}$", for the star points (B).

4 strips, $2\frac{1}{2}$" x $23\frac{5}{8}$", for the medallion frame (F).

$2\frac{1}{4}$"-wide bias strips to total 210", for the binding.

*These squares are cut oversize for ease of handling. They will be trimmed to the proper size after appliqué and embellishment.

Preparing for Appliqué

The Moon Baby Quilt includes twelve appliquéd star centers and an appliquéd center medallion. The star centers finish 4" x 4" square, and the center medallion finishes 18¾" x 18¾". As noted in the cutting instructions on page 22, these squares are cut oversize for ease in handling during appliqué and embellishment, and will be trimmed later.

The Shooting Star block (page 33) introduces the fundamentals of appliqué from preparation to completion, including the latest needle-turn methods for outside points, inside points, and curves come full circle. You'll use the methods learned on this cheery motif to appliqué all of the star centers, and the center medallion.

Can you see a darkened edge around the star? This effect comes from stencil shading (optional), which you will need to do before beginning any appliqué technique. So, before you begin preparing for appliqué, read about stencil shading on page 30. If you plan to ink your appliqué, you might do that in advance as well. If so, refer to page 31.

Preparing the Appliqué Background Squares

Finger-press each 7" x 7" blue or pink star center square (A) in half diagonally in both directions to create an X. This marks the center of the square for placement of the appliqués.

Each pattern is marked with an X to identify its center and its orientation on the background square. The exception is The Moon Baby and Sprinkled Stars (page 36), which you can place by eye on the medallion center.

1. Use pages 33–35 to make 3 Master Pattern pages for the 12 star center appliqué patterns. To do this, photocopy pages 33–35 onto three 8½" x 11" sheets of uncut, self-stick labels (see page 20). Cut the Master Patterns apart to make the 12 squares, and begin with The Shooting Star.

2. Make a "window template" for The Shooting Star pattern by cutting the star shape out from the 4" x 4" photocopied pattern, and setting the star aside. (This will become the Star template.) Tape the initial cut you've made in the window template as shown, but do not remove its peel-off backing.

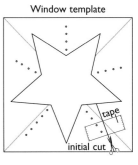

Window template

tape

initial cut

3. Center the window template over the right side of the creased appliqué background square. Use a marking pen or pencil to draw the star $\frac{1}{16}$" inside the cut edge of the window template as shown. This becomes the placement drawing for the star appliqué. The tracing is slightly smaller than the finished appliqué, so the marking will not show.

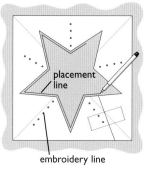

placement line

embroidery line

4. Slit the window template, one dotted line at a time, to mark The Shooting Star's radiating embroidery lines. Study the color photo on page 12 and add similar freehand lines as needed. If you are going to stencil shade the appliqué, turn to page 30 now.

Preparing the Appliqué Motif

1. Cut out the face circle from the Star template, and set the circle aside. (This will become the Face Circle template.) Once again, tape the initial cut. Remove the peel-off backing and press the star template to the right side of the star appliqué fabric as shown. Trace around the star's perimeter to mark the turn line.

Next, trace inside the circle, indicating the placement of the face appliqué. Remove the template.

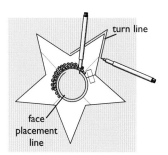

turn line

face placement line

2. Cut out the star appliqué, adding a $\frac{3}{16}$"-wide seam allowance on all sides. Pin the star appliqué to the appliqué background square as shown, aligning the appliqué over the marked placement star.

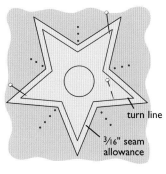

turn line

$\frac{3}{16}$" seam allowance

3. Baste the appliqué in place, using $\frac{1}{4}$"-long stitches, $\frac{1}{4}$" inside the marked turn line. Secure the last stitch before clipping the thread, so that the basting holds firmly.

Stellar Appliqué

This chapter includes the latest techniques for achieving beautifully needleturned inside points, outside points, circles, and curves—all the shapes required to make *The Moon Baby Quilt*'s star centers and center medallion. Once again, The Shooting Star pattern (page 33) is used as the example for the various techniques.

Needleturn Appliqué

1. Thread a milliner's #10 needle with a single strand of thread, 22"-long and knotted at the end. Begin the appliqué by stitching 3/4" before an outside point.

Right-handers start needleturn here.

If you are right-handed, start to the right of a point (outside or inside) and stitch from right to left. If you are left-handed, start to the left of a point and stitch from left to right. The instructions throughout this book are based on right-handed stitching; reverse if you are left-handed.

The star's point above the face is the longest point, and therefore the easiest place to begin.

2. Use your needle to catch the seam allowance, tuck it under the appliqué shape, and pull it toward the appliqué. "Needleturn" the seam under just until the drawn turn line disappears. Hold this folded seam in place, pinched under your left thumb. Bring the needle up from the wrong side of the background block (knot resting underneath), about 3/4" to the right of your thumb. The needle will pierce the background, the turned-under seam, and the appliqué, one needle's width in from the fold.

3. Reinsert the needle into the background block at the same point at which the needle emerged. Scrape the finger beneath the block, then bring the needle back up 1/16" to the left of the previous stitch. Repeat Step 3.

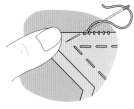

Needleturning an Outside Point

To ensure that the background fabric will not shift as you turn an outside point, pull the background fabric over your left forefinger, holding the fabric taut between your thumb and

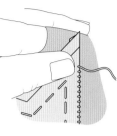

middle finger. Embroiderers call this stabilizing technique "self-hooping."

As you sew the last ¼" of seam at the point, make your stitches very close together (¹/₃₂" apart). Make your last stitch through the turn line right at the point.

The following five steps—*the five Ps*—virtually guarantee perfect points!

1. **Push** a toothpick (or the point of your embroidery scissors) into the seam at the point to grab and control it.

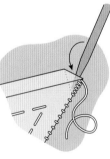

2. **Pivot** the "grabbed" seam down and around to the right until the toothpick is stopped by the right-hand seam. The toothpick turns the point under so emphatically that your last stitches are loosened, as shown.

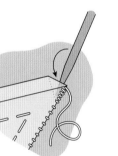

3. **Pinch** your thumb over the corner of the seams you've just tucked under. Pinch in the opposite direction (up and away) from the pivot. This flattens and finger-presses the point.

4. **Pull** the thread at the point out and away from you. The point should slip out, straightening miraculously!

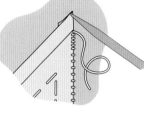

5. **Point** to the point. Take a tiny stitch, entering just inside the appliqué point. Point the needle to the outside edge of the appliqué, emerging through the background only, two threads beyond the appliqué. The needle must pass over the thread emerging from the point. This begins a blanket or lazy daisy stitch.

To finish the stitch, reinsert the needle into the same spot from which it emerged, having passed over the thread loop. Pulled just taut, it creates a perfect point!

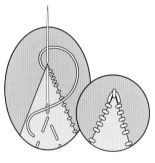

Take similarly close and careful stitches to tuck the left seam under and descend from this point. But first, read what comes next—Needleturning an Inside Point.

Needleturning an Inside Point

1. When your stitches are ½" away from an inside point, cut into, but not beyond, the drawn line at the point. Center the cut, leaving equal seam allowance on each side. Place the needle in the "V" of the slash, its point sandwiched between the appliqué and the background.

2. Pinch your thumb gently over the resulting sandwich. Pull the needle—and thus the seam—down and to the right. The pinching creases the seam under. Pinch until you have stitched up to your thumb.

As seen without the thumb

3. Lift your thumb. Continue stitching until you are ready to take the last stitch before the slash. Three special stitches follow. The first takes a deeper bite out of the fold—two needle-widths deeper (1). The second is a blanket or lazy daisy stitch—three needle-widths deeper (2). After you have needleturned the seam on the left, the third stitch (3) is again deeper, just like the first. These three stitches are like the middle three fingers on your hand: slightly long, longer still, and then slightly longer again.

Coin-Perfect Curves and Circles

Circles and curves appear in many blocks in *The Moon Baby Quilt*, including The Shooting Star, our example block. Use this clip-and-turn method, shared by quiltmaker Cindy Iaia, to make curves and circles as round as a coin. Even circles as tiny as ¼" in diameter finish perfectly, with nice, smooth edges.

1. Without removing the peel-off backing from the face circle template (Step 1, page 24), place the template on the right side of the appliqué fabric, and trace around the circle's perimeter to mark the turn line.

2. Use the template to mark the face circle for embroidery. You can use a sheet of dressmaker's tracing paper to transfer the details.

I prefer to adapt the template by piercing holes, in the center of each eye, cheek, and lip line to create an opening to mark placement lines.

Draw embroidery lines.

Draw what the template allows, then freehand or cut the template further as needed.

3. Cut out the circle appliqué, adding a ⅛"-wide seam allowance. Clip the raw edge every ¼", cutting into, but not beyond, the drawn turn line. Baste the circle to the center of the star with a large X, as shown in Step 4.

4. To needleturn the curve, turn under the first two clipped seam "tabs" and hold them with your thumbnail. Begin stitching at mid-curve. Take a few tiny, close stitches, then needleturn the next tab. Stitch from tab to tab, pausing mid-curve to turn the next tab.

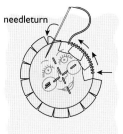

needleturn

Turn under seam allowance.

To avoid creating peaks in a curve, always stop stitching ⅛" before you reach your thumb. Lift your thumb, then needleturn a bit more curve. Use your needle, catching the seam allowance from beneath, working the needle like a windshield wiper to smooth the curve as you go.

Freezer Paper-Inside Appliqué

An alternative to needleturning is preparing appliqué with freezer paper inside. This method speeds the process when you must repeat the same shape (for example, a heart or leaf) multiple times. A fabric shape prepared with this method looks like the finished appliqué. This makes the shape especially useful in design: you can see in advance how the finished product will look. I would not recommend this method for very small or fussy shapes.

Cut a freezer paper template for each appliqué shape. Pin the template, shiny side up, to the wrong side of the appliqué fabric, and then cut out the fabric shape, adding a ¼"-wide seam allowance. Turn and press the seam allowance toward the shiny side of the freezer paper, and you are ready for appliqué.

back of fabric

front of fabric

freezer paper shiny side up

When the appliqué is complete, cut a slit in the background fabric, and carefully remove the paper. *Appliqué 12 Easy Ways* (see book list on page 48) gives more information about this—and other—appliqué techniques.

Edge-Fused Appliqué

Edge-fused appliqué is sturdy and washable, and the unbonded centers invite hand embroidery. Once the appliqués are in place, you can finish the edges either by hand with a blanket stitch, or by machine with a satin or zigzag stitch. If you wish, use the edge-fusing method to appliqué *The Moon Baby Quilt*, or to make the nursery accessories that begin on page 41.

1. Trace the appliqué shape onto the paper side of lightweight fusible web (page 21).

2. Follow the manufacturer's directions to press the fusible web to the wrong side of the appliqué fabric, pressing the outside edges only. Cut out the appliqué exactly on the drawn line. Do not add seam allowance.

3. Place the appliqué web-side down on the background fabric. Follow the manufacturer's directions, again fusing *the edges of the appliqué only.* Do not press further than 1/3" beyond the raw edges of the appliqué.

front of fabric

4. Use a narrow machine satin or zigzag stitch to cover the raw edge with color-matched thread. If you prefer, you can hand appliqué the edge with a fine blanket stitch (page 32). Make stitches 1/16" deep and 1/16" apart, using a single strand of color-matched embroidery floss.

Layered Appliqué

Some blocks include more than one layer of appliqué, so plan the layering sequence before you begin. Some layering sequences, such as the face in The Shooting Star, are easy to spot. Some are not: the horizon appliqué is the top layer in both The Dawn (page 34) and The Dusk (page 34) blocks. For complex blocks such as The Father (page 35) and The Wee

Babe (page 35), simply ask yourself, "What must be appliquéd down first so that its raw edge will be covered by the appliqué layer on top of it?"

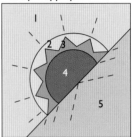

Sample appliqué order

Leave covered edges raw.

Ultrasuede Appliqué

If you refer to the color photos of the blocks on pages 5–17, you can see that Ultrasuede is used for a number of the smaller appliqués. For example, the stars in The Moon Baby and Sprinkled Stars (page 5) are all Ultrasuede, though they could have been stitched in cotton.

Appliquéing Ultrasuede is quick and easy! Because you do not needleturn the edge, you do not need to add a seam allowance to the appliqué shape. Use a glue stick to "baste" the appliqué to the background, then stitch right over the raw edge, using the same thread, needle, and appliqué stitch you would use for a cotton appliqué.

Dimensional Appliqué Accent

One of the blocks, The Mother (page 35), features an apron that adds a touch of dimensional appliqué. To duplicate this effect, cut a 2" x 2²/₃" rectangle of fabric. Roll under and stitch a hem on the two long sides and one short side. Finger-pleat the remaining raw edge. Baste the pleated edge of the apron in place at the mother's waistline, leaving a bit of skirt showing at the hips. Tack the bottom corners of the apron to the skirt, and appliqué a belt.

Whimsical Embellishments

If you study the large color photos accompanying *The Moon Baby Story* (pages 5–17), you will notice a variety of wonderful, whimsical embellishments enhancing the blocks. Refer back to these photos, and to the patterns on pages 33–36, for inspiration and guidance in embellishing your Moon Baby blocks. The following pages tell you how.

Note that stencil shading must be done before appliqué, right after you have slit the window template and marked the embroidery lines (Step 4, page 24), and before you cut out the appliqué shape. Inking can be done in advance also so that, should you err, you have simply to ink again.

Stencil Shading

Stencil shading with oil pastels (page 20) gives appliqué a mysterious beauty. If you expect your quilt will be laundered frequently, eliminate the shading. For a wall quilt, it's delightful! The Shooting Star (page 33), our example throughout, is a perfect block with which to start.

1. Stabilize a 4½" square of yellow star appliqué fabric by ironing a same-size square of freezer paper (shiny side down) to its wrong side.

2. After you've marked the necessary placement lines on the background fabric (Steps 3 and 4, page 24), enlarge the opening in the star window template by cutting off the width of a pencil line all around. Remove the window template's protective backing, and press the template (sticky side down) onto the front side of the appliqué fabric.

3. Mark the turn line onto the appliqué fabric by tracing around the star opening in the window template with a black or brown .01 Pigma pen.

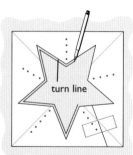

4. The window template is now your artist's palette. Scribble a dime-sized dot each of yellow, orange, and red oil pastel onto the window template, around the perimeter of the star shape.

5. Pull a 5" square muslin scrap over your forefinger. Beginning with the lightest color, push the oil pastel over the edge of the template, onto the appliqué fabric, working the color inward approximately ⅓" or so. Push hardest just inside the edge of the template, and then taper off the pressure until you've achieved the desired shading. Continue in this fashion, scribbling more color on the template as needed, and working from the lightest to the darkest color. Remove the window template and the freezer paper.

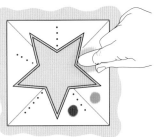

Push color onto fabric.

6. Heat-set the color with a dry iron, using a paper tissue pressing cloth to assure color-fastness in gentle washing. Cut out the appliqué, adding a 3/16"-wide seam allowance. Now you are ready for Step 2 on page 24.

Inking

You also can create the effect of shading by applying dots of ink (also known as pen-and-ink stippling) with a Pigma Micron pen or other permanent pen (page 20). You can see an example on The Moon Baby and Sprinkled Stars center medallion (page 5), where dots have been added to emphasize an interior curve in the cloth of the baby's pajamas.

The written word is also an embellishment. For example, the block Rejoice! (page 16) is inscribed with a Pigma Micron .01 pen in my version of the Copperplate Script.

If you ink before you appliqué, stabilize the wrong side of the appliqué fabric with freezer paper, just as you did for stenciling (page 30). Adhere masking tape to the outlined appliqué as a guideline to write along. Finish any tails of letters that fall below the line after removing the tape.

Take extra care when writing on Ultrasuede. Let the ink dry thoroughly to avoid smearing, and then, using a paper tissue pressing cloth, heat-set it with a dry iron on the synthetic setting.

Refer to *Fancy Appliqué* (see book list on page 48) for the Copperplate Alphabet, and for additional guidance with both inking and calligraphy.

Embroidery

The Moon Baby blocks are greatly enhanced by the addition of embroidery. For example, in The Evening Breeze (page 8), a stem stitch is used to emphasize the curved puff of a cloud. In The Moon Baby and Sprinkled Stars center medallion (page 5), "legged" French knots create some of the babe's curls. All of the stitches are simple—the sort your grandmother may have taught you.

Study the color photo of each block (pages 5–17). Ask yourself: "Which stitch was sewn? What colors and how many strands of floss were used?" Occasionally, to achieve a special

or more subtle effect, a strand of one shade is mixed with a strand of another. I used no more than two strands of floss at a time for any of the embroidery on *The Moon Baby Quilt*. I also used an embroidery hoop to avoid distortion.

The following embroidery stitches appear in the various blocks of *The Moon Baby Quilt*. The block numbers that appear following each stitch refer to the with the pattern numbers on pages 33–36. For more on embroidery, refer to *Elegant Stitches* by Judith Baker Montano (see Sources, page 47).

Blanket Stitch

Used on patterns 3, 4, 5, 6, 7, 8, and 13.

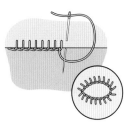

Chain Stitch

Used on patterns 1, 3, 4, 5, 6, 8, 10, 11, 12, and 13.

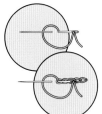

Couching

Used on patterns 2, 4, and 6.

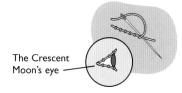

The Crescent Moon's eye

Filler Stitch

Used on pattern 13.

French Knot

Used on patterns 1, 2, 3, 5, 6, 9, 10, 11, and 13.

Lazy Daisy

Used on patterns 2, 10, and 11.

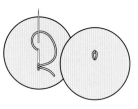

Legged French Knot

Used on pattern 13.

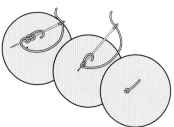

Running Stitch

Used on patterns 1, 2, 5, 7, 8, 10, and 12.

Satin Stitch

Used on patterns 2, 4, 5, 6, 7, and 13.

Stem Stitch

Used on patterns 1 through 13.

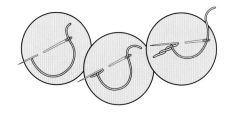

The Patterns

The Shooting Star (1)

The Smiling Sun (2)

The Sleepy Star (3)

The Evening Breeze (4)

33

The Spirit in Bloom (5)   The Crescent Moon (6)

The Dusk (7)   The Dawn (8)

Rejoice! (9)

The Wee Babe (10)

REJOICE!
ELIAS EMERSON
SIENKIEWICZ
BORN MARCH 12
2001

CONCORD,
MASSACHUSETTS

The Father (11)

The Mother (12)

35

The Moon Baby and Sprinkled Stars (13)

Completing the Moon Baby Quilt

Quilt photo on page 19

Finished Size: 50" x 50"

The journey continues after you have appliquéd and embellished the Moon Baby star centers and center medallion. Now you are ready to make the twelve Star blocks and assemble *The Moon Baby Quilt.*

Yardages and cutting instructions for the entire quilt appear on pages 21–22. To make the process quick and easy, cutting and construction uses a variety of no-template, rotary-cutting methods. If rotary cutting is new to you, you'll be thrilled by its efficiency! For an excellent overview, refer to *Rotary Cutting with Alex Anderson* (see Sources, page 47).

Completing the Star Blocks

Finished Size: 8" x 8"

You will need to make four Flying Geese units for the star points in each Star block. Each unit finishes 2" x 4" (2¹/₂" x 4¹/₂" including seam allowances). If you wish, you can "assembly line" or chain piece to speed the piecing process.

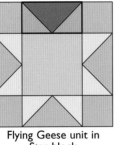
Flying Geese unit in Star block

1. Draw a diagonal line from corner to corner on the wrong side of a gold/yellow B square. Make 8.

2. With right sides together, position a marked square on one end of a blue C rectangle. Stitch along the diagonal line. Trim the excess fabric as shown, leaving a ¹/₄"-wide seam allowance. Open the seam and finger-press. Make 4.

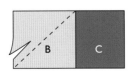

3. Repeat to sew a marked B square to the other end of each B/C unit from Step 2.

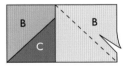

4. Stitch a blue D square to each end of a Flying Geese unit. Make 2.

5. Carefully trim the appliquéd star center (A) to 4¹/₂" x 4¹/₂". Stitch a Flying Geese unit to opposite sides of the star center.

6. Lay out the block as shown. Carefully pin and match the seams, and then sew the rows together to complete the block.

7. Repeat Steps 1–6 to make a total of 12 Star blocks.

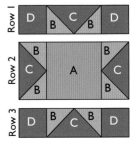

Assembling the Quilt Top

Trim The Moon Baby and Sprinkled Stars center medallion to 19¼" x 19¼". On the wrong side, mark a dot ¼" in from each corner, and then add and miter the medallion frame.

1. Fold each yellow/gold F strip end to end to find the center of the strip. Finger-press the crease.

2. Measure 9⅛" from the crease in both directions, and mark a dot on the wrong side of the strip, ¼" from the edge.

3. Use a ruler to draw a line from the dot to the outer edge of the border at a 45° angle. Repeat at each end of all 4 of the F strips.

4. With right sides together, match the center of a strip to the center of the medallion, and the dots on the strip with the corner dots on the medallion; pin.

5. Sew from dot to dot, stopping ¼" from each end of the strip. Repeat to add strips to all 4 sides.

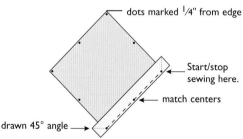

dots marked ¼ from edge

Start/stop sewing here.

match centers

drawn 45° angle

6. Fold the medallion on the diagonal as shown, aligning the 45° markings on adjacent strips.

7. Sew from the dot out to the edge of the strip. Open the seam and press it flat. Trim the excess fabric, leaving

folded edge

a ½"-wide seam allowance. Repeat for all 4 corners.

8. Refer to the quilt photo on page 19 and the quilt layout on page 22. Sew the Star blocks together in the following pairs:

The Mother and The Evening Breeze (upper right corner); The Dawn and The Sleeping Star (lower right corner); The Smiling Sun and The Shooting Star (lower left corner); and The Father and The Dusk (upper left corner).

9. Sew an outside setting triangle (G) to opposite sides of each paired-star unit from Step 8. Refer to the diagram below and the quilt layout on page 22, to be certain you are positioning the triangles correctly. You'll notice that the triangles have been cut oversize. This allows the Star blocks to "float" in the outside border.

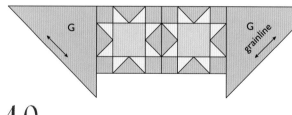

10. Sew an inside setting triangle (H) to adjacent sides of each remaining Star block. Refer to the diagram at right and the quilt layout on page 22, to be certain you are positioning the triangles correctly.

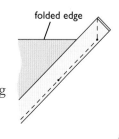

> **T**o avoid distorting the bias edges when sewing the setting triangles to the Star blocks, sew with the blocks on top and the triangles against the feed dogs. The feed dogs help feed the bias edges more evenly.

11. Refer to the quilt photo on page 19 and the quilt layout on page 22. Sew the 4 units made in Step 10 to the medallion, positioning them as shown.

12. Sew the 4 units made in Step 9 to the appropriate corners of the quilt top, matching the center seam of the star units with the mitered corners of the medallion frame.

13. Match the center of a corner setting triangle (I) to the center seam of each star unit added in Step 12. Pin, then sew the triangles to the quilt. If desired, trim excess fabric, leaving a 1/4"-wide seam allowance.

Finishing the Quilt

Mark the quilt top with a design of your choice. Layer the quilt top, batting, and backing; baste. Quilt as desired. Quilting around the edges of the stars emphasizes the star points. The large outside corner triangles of the quilt provide a wonderful place to show off your quilting skills. Bind the edges with a 2¼"-wide bias strip.

Making a Special Label for Your Quilt

Take the time to create a lovely cloth label for your quilt, and appliqué the label to your quilt after it is quilted and bound. A label confirms the origin of the quilt: who made it, for whom, when, and where. If the quilt is a gift, this special label can also convey the quilt's intent with heartwarming sentiment.

You may choose to hand- or machine-embroider the label, type the words, or write them by hand with a permanent pen. Modern technology offers additional simple alternatives. Using June Tailor Colorfast Printer Fabric Sheets to put my words and a photo on cloth,

I transformed the entire quilt back into a veritable "site" for charming and inspiring things to read and share with my special child. I appliquéd the label shown on page 40, plus *The Moon Baby Story* in its entirety. I added a copy of the classic children's poem *Wynken, Blynken, and Nod* by Eugene Field as an alternative bedtime story. The texts were typed on the computer. I added one more item: a framed color photo of the quilt's recipient, Wee Elias, cradled by his big sister Ellie. Each of these items was neatly bordered with an appliqué frame.

The Moon Baby Quilt label

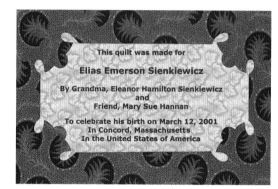

This quilt was made for

Elias Emerson Sienkiewicz

By Grandma, Eleanor Hamilton Sienkiewicz
and
Friend, Mary Sue Hannan

To celebrate his birth on March 12, 2001
In Concord, Massachusetts
In the United States of America

With a bit of experimentation, I found a way to add color and visual texture to an otherwise unexciting white label. I made a color photocopy of a yellow print fabric and used that color photocopy as the 8½" x 11" paper on which to print words from the computer. Similarly, I used a color photocopy of a photograph to print the photo I framed for the back of the quilt. For more about photo transfer techniques, refer to *The Photo Transfer Handbook* by Jean Ray Laury (see Sources, page 47).

Alternate Color Schemes for The Moon Baby Quilt

The Moon Baby Quilt as shown on pages 19 and 41 and pictured throughout the previous pages, demonstrates just one of many possible color schemes for this special quilt.

The photo and illustration below suggest an alternate colorway for additional inspiration. Enjoy interpreting the design in colors that suit the nursery of your own special babe.

The Moon Baby and Sprinkled Stars center medallion.
Made by Charlene Dakin, based on
Elly Sienkiewicz's patterns.

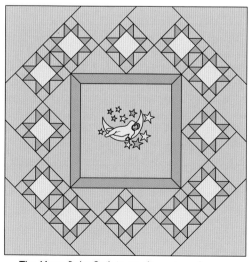

The Moon Baby Quilt in an alternate colorway

Stellar Moon Baby Nursery

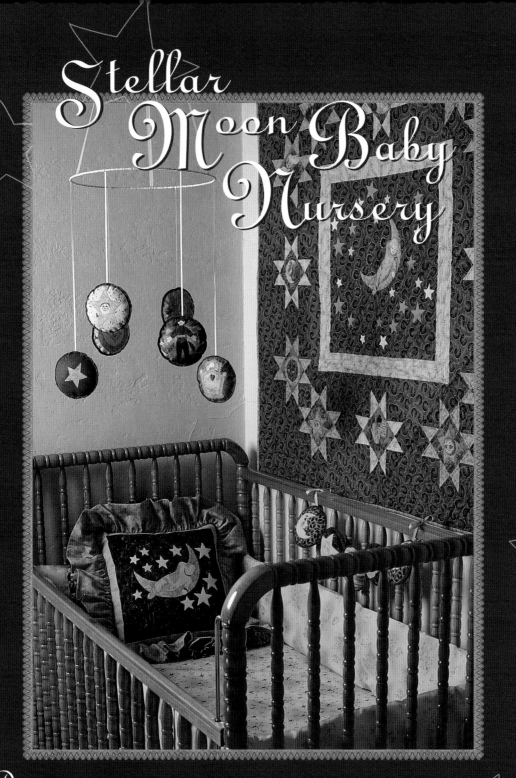

$\mathcal{D}$evelop an entire nursery theme around *The Moon Baby Quilt* blocks, or make a special gift for a new mother. Use a single Moon Baby appliqué, or combine your favorites to make one or all of these charming nursery accessories.

Refer to the block patterns on pages 33–36, and your favorite appliqué and embellishment techniques beginning on page 25. For quick results, edge-fuse, then embroider the appliqués.

Golden Slumbers

Golden Slumbers, 28½" x 37½". Made by Lynda Carswell, based on Elly Sienkiewicz's appliqué pattern.

Golden Slumbers features Attic Window blocks in a classic set, with a single appliqué—The Moon Baby. Create a dimensional effect by using a darker print for the left frame of the window and a lighter print for the bottom frame.

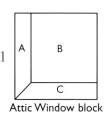

Attic Window block

Supplies

Medium-dark gold print: ⅓ yard for the left frame (A)

Medium-light gold print: ⅓ yard for the bottom frame (C)

Assorted dark-blue and black prints: scraps (at least 7½" x 7½" and 1 scrap 9" x 9") to total ⅞ yard for the window pane (B)

Assorted gold, pink, and flesh-toned prints and solids: 6" x 6" scraps for the appliqué

Purple print: ⅞ yard for the sashing and borders

Blue print: 1 yard for the backing

Black solid: ½ yard for the binding

Batting: 31" x 41"

Optional: Scraps of lightweight fusible web for edge-fused appliqué

Cutting

From the medium-dark gold, cut 12 rectangles, 2" x 9⅜", for the left frame (A). Trim the end at a 45° angle as shown.

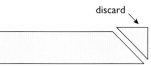

From the medium-light gold, cut 12 rectangles, 2" x 9⅜", for the bottom frame (C). Trim the end at a 45° angle as shown.

From the dark-blue and black prints, cut 11 squares, 7½" x 7½", for the window panes (B); and 1 square, 9" x 9", for the appliquéd pane (B).

From the purple fabric, cut 8 strips, 1" x 9" for the vertical sashing (D); 3 strips, 1" x 27", for the horizontal sashing (E); 2 strips, 1¼" x 36", for the side borders (F); and 2 strips, 1¼" x 28½", for the top and bottom borders (G).

Assembling the Blocks

1. Reduce to 73% the Moon Baby and Sprinkled Stars pattern on page 36. Use your preferred method to appliqué The Moon Baby onto the 9" x 9" square (B), embellishing as desired. When you've finished, carefully trim the block to 7$\frac{1}{2}$" x 7$\frac{1}{2}$".

2. Stitch A and C to B, mitring the frame as shown. Press the mitered corners open.

Assembling the Quilt Top

1. Refer to the quilt layout (right) to arrange and stitch 4 rows of Attic Windows blocks, inserting the vertical sashing strips (D). Press toward the sashing.

2. Sew the rows together, inserting the horizontal sashing strips (E). Press toward the sashing.

3. Stitch border strips (F) to the sides of the quilt. Press toward the borders. Stitch border strips (G) to the top and bottom. Press toward the borders.

Finishing the Quilt

Layer the quilt top, batting, and backing; baste. Quilt as desired. Bind the edges with 142"-long bias strip, 2$\frac{1}{4}$" wide, of black solid, and add a label (pages 39–40) to finish.

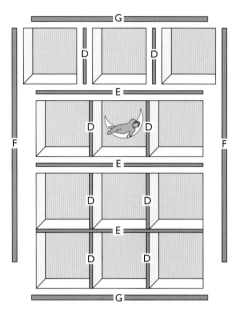

Golden Slumbers quilt layout

The Moon Baby Mobile

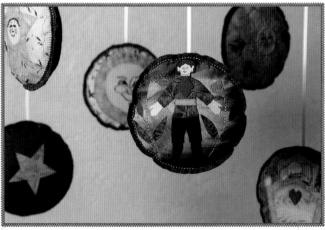

Designed by Kerry Smith. Made by Charlene Dakin, based on Elly Sienkiewicz's appliqué patterns.

A mobile safely hung above the crib helps guide a child off to dreamland. Our sample was made using the edge-fused appliqué technique (page 28), but you can use any technique that suits your fancy. For an additional photo, see page 41.

Supplies

Assorted blue prints: Scraps (at least 8" x 8") to total $\frac{1}{2}$ yard for the appliqué background squares

Blue, pink, yellow, gold, orange, red, green, and flesh-toned prints and solids:
6" x 6" scraps for the appliqués

Blue felt: ³/₈ yard, 45"-wide for the felt circles

Yellow/gold felt or fabric: ¹/₈ yard for the stars on the back of the felt pillows

¹/₈"-wide white ribbon: 2⁵/₈ yards to hang the felt pillows

⁵/₈"-wide white ribbon: 3 yards to wrap the wreath form

³/₈"-wide white ribbon: 2³/₄ yards to hang the mobile

Six-strand embroidery floss

Cotton balls or fiberfill

Lightweight fusible web

14" wire wreath form

Craft glue

Cup hook

Cutting

Star pattern

From the assorted blue prints, cut 6 squares, 8" x 8", for the appliqué background squares.

From the blue felt, cut 12 circles, 5" in diameter, for the felt circles.

From the yellow/gold felt or fabric, cut 6 stars, using the pattern on this page, for the back of the felt pillows.

From the ¹/₈"-wide ribbon, cut two 12"-lengths, two 14"-lengths, and two 18"-lengths, to hang the felt pillows.

From the ³/₈"-wide ribbon, cut three 30"-lengths to hang the mobile.

Assembly

1. Refer to the patterns on pages 33–35, and use your preferred technique to appliqué a favorite Moon Baby motif onto a background square, embellishing as desired. Trim each

square to a 4¹/₂"-diameter circle, and appliqué it to a blue felt circle. Make 6.

2. Hand or machine stitch each felt circle from Step 1 to a plain felt circle, right sides out. Pause while stitching to knot one end of a length of ¹/₈"-wide ribbon, and insert it into the seam at the top of the circle. Cut a 1¹/₂" slit in the center of each of the plain felt circles, and stuff the "pillows" fully with cotton balls or fiberfill.

3. Edge-fuse a yellow star to each plain felt circle, covering the slit.

Back (slit covered by star)   Front

4. Glue one end of the ⁵/₈"-wide ribbon to the wire wreath form. Wrap the ribbon around the wire, covering it completely. Secure the end with glue.

5. Wrap the loose end of each ¹/₈"-wide ribbon over the wreath form, outside to inside, 7¹/₂" apart, and stitch the ribbon to itself. Wrap the 3 lengths of ³/₈"-wide ribbon under the wreath form, outside to inside, 15" apart, and stitch the ribbon to itself.

6. Tie the free end of the ³/₈"-wide ribbons together in a loop, and hang the mobile on the cup hook to check for balance. Adjust the ribbons as necessary, and trim the excess. If desired, tie additional ribbon into a bow around the base of the loop to hide the knot.

The Moon Baby Crib Decoration

Designed by Kerry Smith. Made by Charlene Dakin, based on Elly Sienkiewicz's appliqué patterns.

Choose five Moon Baby appliqués to create this festive crib decoration. Assemble the same supplies needed for *The Moon Baby Mobile* (pages 43–44), cutting enough fabric and felt for five pillows instead of six. Omit the ribbons, wreath form, glue, and cup hook, and add 1⅓ yards of ⅜"-wide ribbon, cut into two 24"-long pieces.

Assembly

1. Follow Steps 1–3 on page 44, making 5 pillows instead of 6. Instead of inserting knotted ribbon into each pillow, fold the pieces of ⅜"-wide ribbon in half, and insert the folded end into the top of 2 pillows.

2. Tack the pillows together with a few whipstitches, keeping the pillows with ribbons on opposite ends. Tie the end ribbons to the crib.

The Moon Baby and Sprinkled Stars Pillow

Designed by Kerry Smith. Made by Charlene Dakin, based on Elly Sienkiewicz's appliqué pattern.

Create an inviting "nest" in the nursery rocker with the addition of this comfy pillow.

Supplies

Blue print: ½ yard for the appliqué background

Pink, brown, yellow, and flesh-toned prints and solids: 6" x 6" scraps for the appliqués

Blue stripe: ¼ yard for the inner border

Dark-blue print: 1⅝ yards for the pillow back and wide ruffle

Red print: ½ yard for the cording

Gold print: 1⅛ yards for the narrow ruffle

2 yards cotton/polyester cording, ¼" diameter

Six-strand embroidery floss

Pearl cotton #5

14" zipper to match the backing

16" x 16" pillow form

Optional: 3" x 3" scraps of Ultrasuede for the appliqués; ½ yard lightweight fusible web for edge-fused appliqué.

Cutting

From the blue print fabric, cut 1 square, 15" x 15", for the appliqué background.

From the blue stripe, cut 2 strips, 2½" x 14", for the side borders; and 2 strips, 2½" x 17", for the top and bottom borders.

From the dark-blue print, cut 1 rectangle, 17" x 5", for the pillow back; 1 rectangle, 17" x 14", for the pillow back; and 4 strips, 10" x width of the fabric, for the wide ruffle.

From the red print fabric, cut 1 square, 15" x 15", for the cording.

From the gold print, cut 4 strips, 9" x width of the fabric, for the narrow ruffle.

Assembly

All seams are ½" wide unless otherwise noted.

1. Use your preferred method to appliqué the Moon Baby and Sprinkled Stars center medallion (page 36) to the blue print background square, embellishing as desired. Trim the square to 14" x 14".

2. With right sides together, sew the side borders to the appliquéd square. Press the seams toward the border. Repeat to add the top and bottom borders; press.

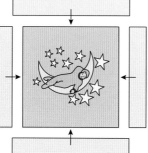

3. Place the pillow-back rectangles right sides together, aligned on the long edge. Machine-baste a ½"-wide seam along the edge. Press the seam open. Use a zipper foot to install the zipper along the seam. Trim the back to 17" x 17". Open the zipper.

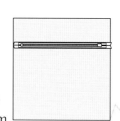

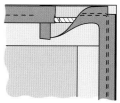

4. Create cording from a 1½" x 70" bias strip, cut from red print fabric. Machine-baste the cording to the pillow front, just inside the ½" seamline. Ease the corners (cutting a notch), and trim the extra cording/bias strip so the cording ends abut and the raw edge of the fabric is covered inside a folded end of the bias.

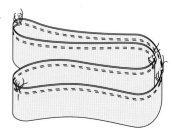

5. For the narrow ruffle, sew the gold print strips together end to end and trim to make a 128"-long strip. Sew the ends together. Fold the strip in half lengthwise, wrong sides together, and press. Divide the strip into 4 sections and mark with pins. Sew a gathering stitch ⅜" from the long raw edge. Gather, removing pins. Repeat with the dark-blue print strips to make the wide ruffle.

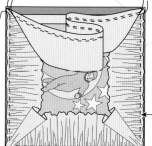

6. Pin the gathered narrow ruffle to the right side of the pillow front, raw edges even. Gather the ruffle to fit, arranging the gathers evenly and easing extra fullness at the corners. Baste the ruffle in place, ⅜" from the raw edges.

7. Pin the gathered wide ruffle on top of the gathered narrow ruffle, raw edges even. Gather, arrange, pin, and baste as for the narrow ruffle. Machine stitch both ruffles and the cording in place, ⅜" from the raw edges.

8. Pin the pillow front to the pillow back, right sides together. Sew the layers together on all 4 sides, ½" from the raw edges. Trim excess fabric from the corners. Turn the cover right side out, insert the pillow form, and zip closed.

More Ideas For Your Moon Baby

Select your favorite Moon Baby appliqués and add them to ready-made items, or to items you make using a commercial pattern. With a bit of craft glue or paint, and a little imagination, you can apply appliqués to lampshades or window treatments, or transfer the designs to a stencil and add fanciful borders to the nursery walls.

Sources

The Elly Sienkiewicz Appliqué Academy® LLC
Bette Augustine, Administrator
41195 Toledo Drive
Hemet, CA 92544
(909) 658-4260
bette@gtemail.net
www.ellysienkiewicz.com
Send $1 for current event brochure. Website lists Elly's upcoming teaching engagements. Requests to Bette for Elly's teaching prospectus will be forwarded to Elly.

Book List
vze34mcn@verizon.net
Email for complete info on Elly's out-of-print books, their availability and prices.

Quilt Adventures
Cynthia Williford
596 E. Danskin Drive
Boise, ID 83716
(208) 433-8500
www.quiltadventures.com
For Elly's designer fabrics and books, and for hand-dyed silk ribbons and floss, and the latest in quilt supplies

Sunset Silhouette Designs
39 Allen Drive
Oroville, WA 98844
www.sunsetsilhouette.com
sunsetsil@aol.com
For an excellent selection of Ultrasuede

Mare's Bears Quilt Shop,
528 Savannah Road
Lewes, DE 19958
(302) 644-0556
maresbears@ce.net
www.maresbearsquiltshop.com
For June Tailor Colorfast Printer Fabric Sheets, Elly's designer fabrics, books, and information about Appliqué by the Sea, where Elly often teaches

Heartbeat Quilts
765 Main Street
Hyannis, MA 02601
(800) 393-8050
www.heartbeatquilts.com
For Elly's designer fabrics and books, and information about Heartbeat Quilt Camp on Cape Cod, where Elly often teaches

Cotton Patch Mail Order
3405 Hall Lane, Dept. CTB
(800) 835-4418
quiltusa@yahoo.com
www.quiltusa.com
For quilting supplies

C&T Publishing, Inc.
P.O. Box 1456
Lafayette, CA 94549
Phone: (800) 284-1114
ctinfo@ctpub.com
www.ctpub.com

For a free catalog and more information about the following books, or many of Elly's books listed on page 48:

Art of Classic Quiltmaking, The, Harriet Hargrave and Sharyn Craig

Elegant Stitches, Judith Baker Montano

Photo Transfer Handbook, The, Jean Ray Laury

Rotary Cutting with Alex Anderson, Alex Anderson

About the Author

Photo by Donald Hamilton Sienkiewicz

Elly Sienkiewicz studied art, religion, and history at Wellesley College, but she already cherished the idea of being a grandmother. She earned a Masters of Science in History and Education, taught social studies, met and married Stan Sienkiewicz, and settled in Washington, D.C. Between the birth of her two sons, Donald Hamilton and Alex Corbly, she learned quiltmaking—at first by phone—from her great-aunt Atha in West Virginia. Daughter Eileen Katherine (Katya) was born a few years later.

As the children grew, Elly's quiltmaking evolved. She taught quiltmaking from her home; for seven years ran a quilt shop by mail; and in 1983 wrote her first book, *Spoken Without a Word.*

Elly's popularity as a national teacher grew. Time passed: her eldest, Donald, married another Katja (Hock), and, within a few years, Elly received a phone call, "Eleanor Naomi Sienkiewicz was born this day." Not only had Elly become a grandmother, but she also had a namesake!

When Little Ellie was two years old, word came that she would have a brother. That's when Grandma Elly started "seeing" a baby in the moon. Wee Elias Emerson Sienkiewicz is the inspiration for *The Moon Baby Story* and quilt. At this writing, Elias, now two, has a new baby sister, Davina Teresa Sienkiewicz. Grandma Elly, Ellie, and Elias are all pictured here with Davina, just 23 hours old. Doesn't Grandma Elly look like a lady whose dream has come true?

Sixteen other books by Elly Sienkiewicz:

Appliqué 12 Borders and Medallions
Appliqué 12 Easy Ways
Appliqué a Paper Greeting!
Baltimore Album Legacy
Baltimore Album Quilts
Baltimore Album Revival
Baltimore Beauties and Beyond, Part I
Baltimore Beauties and Beyond, Part II

Best of Baltimore Beauties, Vol. I
Best of Baltimore Beauties, Vol. II
Design a Baltimore Album Quilt
Dimensional Appliqué
Fancy Appliqué
Papercuts and Plenty, Baltimore Beauties and Beyond, Vol. III
Romancing Ribbons into Flowers
Spoken Without a Word